The Roots Beneath The Tree

A Book of Poetry

ASHLEY RAQUELLE

The Roots Beneath the Tree: A Book of Poetry

Ashley Raquelle Creations LLC

2991 Sacramento Street

Unit 269

Berkeley, CA 94702

ManifestRealitiesHC.com/books-ashleyraquelle

Check out Poetry by Ashley Raquelle on YouTube.com/@lifeisrocqi

ISBN: 979-8-218-43987-3

Chapter Title Page Art by JDE2

Check out @jde2creates

"Towering trees grow from the tiniest seeds."

Ashley Raquelle

DEDICATION

Power. Magic. Beauty.

Words create life.

Words paint a picture.

Words are the light, when life goes dark.

Ashley Raquelle

CONTENTS

ACKNOWLEDGMENTS

The chapter, “Seeds of the Tree,” is dedicated to Ms. Knapp, my eighth grade Language Arts Teacher at Thurmont Middle School. Language Arts or English classes always came easily for me. I read the books. I wrote the papers. I even helped my peers. It wasn’t until Ms. Knapp’s class that I started to not do so well. That was because Ms. Knapp challenged me, challenged my writing, to think in ways I hadn’t before. I grew tremendously from that experience; especially since that was when I really started writing poetry. After her class, I took a summer writing workshop at Walkersville Middle School, to strengthen my skills some more. I am thankful to all of my English teachers in high school as well who supported me on my writing journey; especially Mr. Headley who informed me about writing contests and was the editor of the school newspaper.

The chapter, “The Ripening of the Fruit,” is dedicated to my parents. Mom, Dad – You supported me in so many ways. You encouraged my growth in this craft. You provided me with opportunities and resources to strengthen my writing. I entered contests, and you were there when I won the awards. I performed my poetry, and you were there cheering me on. You allowed me to explore and practice this, and I am forever grateful. You started me on this journey. During potty training, you had me on the potty, reading a book about potty training. My first toddler bed was a house where the shutters were a bookshelf. You paid for the advanced reading course outside of school to guarantee I fell in love with reading. You took me to the Black owned bookstore chain, Karibu Books, where I could see Black authors, Black characters, and Black stories. You bought me Addy, an American Girl doll, and all the book collections that came with her. You gave me my Barbie dolls; my dolls were the characters in my first story. You allowed my imagination to expand, and you were there when I read it all to you. You permitted me to go to a two-week writing program miles away from home where I was able to work with professional writers in poetry, fiction, and journalism; and then you came to see the showcase displaying what we had learned. The amount of gratitude I feel for you both is tremendous. I would not be in this place, at this moment, with this published book, if it weren't for you. Thank you.

I also want to shout out the era that I was in; 90's and 2000's. I was ALWAYS in my school's library. The Scholastic Book Fair was my favorite time of year. Pizza Hut gave free pizza for reading. And they had commercials like *Zoobooks* encouraging reading and learning about other species. Not to mention *Reading Rainbow* with LeVar Burton. It definitely was a different time compared to now. Although, I was surprised to just learn that *Ranger Rick Zoobooks* magazines, the Book It! Program with Pizza Hut, and the Scholastic Book Fair all still continue to exist today!

I want to give a special acknowledgement to my editor, Ngozi Alston. We met in an English class at our alma mater, Hampton University. While she received her B.A. in English/Liberal Arts, I was completing my minor in English. Ngozi – I am so thankful for having you as my editor; providing insight for clarity, suggestions for grammar, and enthusiasm for my writing. Thank you.

I want to give a special acknowledgement to the visual artist of my chapter title pages, Jamese Evans – JDE2. We both attended Hampton University together. Thank you so much for allowing my words to inspire your art and being a part of this journey with me.

For the Ancestors…

For **Phyllis Wheatley**.
For Ida B. Wells, Zora Neale Hurston, and Maya Angelou.
For **Langston Hughes**, Lorraine Hansberry, and **James Baldwin**.
For Gwendolyn Brooks, Audre Lorde, and Octavia Butler.
For **Harriet Tubman** and Sojourner Truth.
For Michael Jackson.
For Nina Simone, Countee Cullen, and Gwen Ifill.
For John Lewis. For Huey P. Newton.
For W.E.B. DuBois and Booker T. Washington. For Marcus Garvey.
For Rev. Dr. Martin Luther King Jr. For Malcolm X.

For the Elders –
For **Alice Walker**, **Angela Davis**, and Oprah Winfrey.
For Sister Souljah and Erykah Badu.
For Nikki Giovanni. For Bobby Seale.
For President Barack Obama.
For Sonia Sanchez.
For **Mildred D. Taylor**, **Sharon M. Draper**, and **Sharon G. Flake**.

TIMELINE

Seeds of the Tree

When I first started writing poetry in eighth grade, through ninth grade. 2005-2007

The Flowers that Blossomed

From sophomore year of high school to junior year. 2008-2009

- I performed “From Darkness to Light.”
- I won an award in a writing contest for “From Darkness to Light.”

The Ripening of the Fruit

My senior year of high school. 2009-2010.

- I performed “Man in the Mirror” and “The Nightmare That Was Reality: Memories of the Middle Passage.”
- I performed “Tick, Tock…It’s Graduation Time” at my high school graduation.
- I won 1st place in a writing contest for “My Eight Letter Word.”

Sweet Cherries and Plums Plucked

From 7th grade to my senior year of high school. 2005-2010.

I wanted this book to show the progression of my writing as I grew in my adolescence, experienced life, and learned more of my craft. Please keep in mind my age at the time I wrote these poems as you are reading. This is my first poetry book. My second book of poetry will be poems from my young adulthood.

Thank you for reading.

Ashley Raquelle

Seeds of the Tree

THE CATERPILLAR

I am not like everyone else.
No,
I am different.
I crawl on leaves,
I cannot taste the splendid goodness.
My friends do.

Why doesn't the bird glance my way?
He does with my friends.
They used to be like me,
Fat, long, and ugly.
Now they are thin and beautiful.
While I remain the same.
Who do you think the bird will choose?
My friends who are perfect,
Or the "beauty in her own way" girl?

I admire my friends and hope to be like them someday.
Although, some of my friends, arrogant about their beauty,
The bird chooses them and teaches them a lesson.

I would rather be me – not perfect in any shape or form.
But real.
True.

Unique.
A leader who follows her own path.
The one who has natural beauty,
That is much more powerful than hiding behind a fake face.
One day I will spread my wings and fly.
I will look to the sun,
And not wait for the bird.
I will be me.
Everyone will love me for that.
I will not change myself or show off,
Like my friends do.
I will be me,
And only me.

CAN I FLY WITHOUT WINGS?

The wind never vents through my dress of feathers.
The surrounding storm swallows me whole,
And I can longer see the stars to guide my way.
Can I fly without wings?

His gentle lips have not pecked mine,
For the path to my heart has not been opened.
How can I flutter across a sea full of fear?
For I have no island of courage.
Can I fly without wings?

My pillow of hope has fallen off the bed,
But I do not ache with sorrow.
I can soar across the sea without drowning.
The ocean will not take me under.
Without any wings, could I still fly?

Yes…

I'll fly across the sky.

IS IT EVEN POSSIBLE?

Is it even possible to find what I've been looking for?
My perfect sunset.
The one that warms my heart,
And makes my smile shine.

Is it even possible to find my fantasies in real life?
My perfect story.
Where I don't have to read about my guy,
And I can see the love within his eyes.

Is it even possible to find my perfect harmony?
Where the notes write themselves.
And I don't have to wait any longer
To finally listen to the song of love.

Is it even possible…
That this could be reality,
And not all a dream.
That my fantasies aren't blending into real life,
Blurring my eyes from the truth?

Is it even possible…
That this could be "the one,"
And I don't have to wait 'til college
To find him?

Is it even possible…
That this could be love?
I don’t even know what love is;
Does anybody know, and if so, could they tell me?

Is it even possible…
That my late-night phone calls turn into something more?
That my previous bad relationship caused this friendship to form?
And that I might actually have a long, worthwhile relationship?

Is it even possible…
That this could be love?

LOST IDENTITY

I am who I am,
But what does that mean?

Some people believe where you come from
tells the story of your past, present, and future.

And as I learn about my ancestors and my history,
I learn about myself,
But then I know nothing.

For what is my history, my culture, my heritage?
Enslavement?
Civil Rights Movement?
Hip Hop?
Rap?
I don't know,
For my heritage was stolen from me,
Before I was even born.
Who am I?

Am I the beats flowing from a drum on the Ghanaian coast?
Am I the waves that crash against the Brazilian shore?
Am I the dreadlocks that fall down a Jamaican's back?
I don't know.

What I do know is, I am Black.
The way I dress,
The way I talk,
What music I listen to,
The food I eat…

That's my culture.
The culture we invented – recreated, assimilated, forced, didn't know African, stripped.

So, where am I from?
Where do I go?
That's who I am.

The Flowers That Blossomed

MY DEEPEST FEAR

In my dream,

I had not reached my goal.

And I ended up on the streets,

In the freezing cold.

Fear snuck up on me,

And sent shivers down my spine.

But then, I realized that this was your dream…

Not mine.

THE RUPTURE

The crisp fall leaves crinkle under your feet as you walk lightly about.

The cool air fills your lungs with life and clears your head.

Birds are singing on the tree branches nearby.

You feel a gentle calm surrounding you.

The soothing forest circles the frozen pond,

Showing that it's only for you.

The sun shines peacefully through the trees as you slide the skates onto your feet.

You put one foot steadily onto the ice, not knowing if you'll fall.

Everything seems to be fine.

Your second foot comes onto the ice

and you stand pregnant with excitement of all the possibilities that could occur.

You glide onto the ice,

The wind combing through your hair.

You seem to be in a dream,

Where you don't think about the past or the future,

Just being in that moment.

You spread your arms out wide,

The wind carries you,

Not letting you fall.

You hold your head high and close your eyes,

Believing that this dream will never end…

The sky starts to darken and the wind picks up speed,

The trees bow to the murderous wind,

The wind no longer protecting you.

You skid your skates to a stop and strain to see the clear blue sky,

But the tornado of leaves blurs your vision.

Thunder explodes around you,

Followed by a low rumble coming from deep within the Earth.

The ground starts to shake,

A cold deadly scream pierces through the dark sky as the ice is sliced into two.

Your leg falls into one of the cracks,

The ice-cold water pulling you into its deadly arms.

You reach for something to hold onto,

But the wind no longer knows that you're there.

The water drags you further in,

Shoving its coldness into your body.

Tears stream from your eyes,

Not knowing what to do.

No one can hear your screams for help.

The water pushes its hot chilling breath down your throat.

The wind stops its roaring just enough for someone to hear your final scream.

Is it too late to be saved?

THE BATTLEFIELD

Got my armor on,
Guns at the ready,
Ready to take them on.

Why can't I just walk in and relax?
No, I have to go in on the defense.

First step inside,
Whispered insults attack me.
The ones said out right
Don't even offend me.
I can't see the racist words anymore.
I smile and shrug my shoulders;
In my head,
I'm just saying, "One year more."

History class,
Civil War's the lesson.
In order to call me "Black,"
I had to give my blessing.

Move up to Civil Rights,
Heads turns straight to me,
Man, just cut out the lights.

And I'm Black, so what?
I gotta know every name of every Black person
Down the street that came.
And the fact that I'm Black,
What my dog gotta be too?
Like everything I own gotta be black, not blue.

And get the heck out of my hair,
I ain't your little nigger baby doll.
Just because it's different, don't mean you gotta
Run your fingers through it all.
Accept the fact, my hair ain't like yours,
And who gives a crap,
If I got it from the store?

And get off my back
About the way we dance.
We're just being free from our problems,
Give the music a chance.
If we wanted to do something else, that's another place and time.
Just because your dancing doesn't let the beat flow through,
Doesn't make me ashamed of mine.

And yes, I said, "we,"

As in me and Black folk.
But then suddenly, I'm the racist joke.
God says we're human before race,
But not in America,
Where Whites only see the color of your face.

When you don't get your way,
We're being racist against you,
And yet us being "human" took years to come true.

We have BET, Black History Month and so on,
And you want one too.
I mean dang, you have everything.
Just let us have a few!
You might not know how the other half lives,
Even if you do live in a "diverse" area,
Making laws without knowing us is not yours to give.

Barack Hussein Obama is the president,
The first Black one.
I don't want to come to school challenging everything he does
Before he's even begun.
Leave the man alone and let him do his job.
He's better than the last one, and you know it.
The country's pride, now he did rob.

And you wonder why we attend Black colleges,
Cause we're sick of dealing with you.
I'm tired of having to explain everything,
And there, they would've already knew.
I want to take off this armor,
And stop debating every single thing.
Culture and diversity are what I want life to bring.

TRUE LOVE NEVER DIES

On the outside, I'm a shell,
Not letting you in.
But on the inside, I'm a baby,
Reaching for your hand.
I can't do this anymore,
Acting like I don't want you.
I want to let go,
But I can't bid you adieu.

I'm tired of searching,
Because you are found.
I'm tired of my heart hurting,
Because you're not around.
Why do I need you?
Why do I care?
Why is my smile dimmer
Because you're not there?

I can stand on my own two feet
And look the world in the eye.
But just one thought of you,
And I begin to cry.
Tears of happiness we've shared,
Time and time again.

Memories of us together appear
Every now and then.

Take off this hold you have on me,
That's a curse and a blessing.
To have such love in life and it disappear –
Is really quite depressing.
My world was brighter
With you by my side.
But get over you? It's not happening.
And believe me, I've tried.

I don't need a man to be happy,
I can live life on my own.
No one said you can't have fairytale endings
Even if you do end up alone.
But when I'm in your arms,
It's perfection in an embrace.
I thought you felt the same
With that look, upon your face.

You made me laugh.
You made me cry.
I still love you,
And I don't know why.

I meant what I said
About being with you the rest of my life.
I thought you meant what you said,
About me becoming your future wife.

Your feelings now are unknown to me,
But I wish you felt the same.
Make the world disappear except for us,
So gone would be the heartache and pain.
Every guy wants something,
I look at new ones with disgust.
You might have been the same,
But deep down, I know it was more than just lust.

Is it the truth
Or is it a lie
When they say
True love never dies?

MISS CUSTODIAN

Better bring that broom and dust pan,
Get that mop and bucket too.
Throw them rags over your shoulder,
The suds on your hands,
And roll them sleeves up high.
Time to get down on your knees and get to scrubbing that floor.
"Gonna take a serious spit-shine to get dis place clean."
Time's a-wasting, so you better get to getting,
Don't want nobody cooking that filth.

Rewind to hours before…
With that little girl gazing at
That big ole Melting Pot.
"I'm making America," she says,
Staring at her ingredients.
1 cup *White*,
A quarter *Black*.
The rest…she don't know about.

Hispanics who Black,
Hispanics who White,
African Americans with no African in them.
Whites from Kenya,
Blacks from England.

Puerto Rican ain't a race, you better pick one.
Where do they all belong?

But White, is a color,
Black is too.
Where your ancestors from?
Europe, Asia, or Africa?
What are you?

<u>Fast forward, now play.</u>
The pot boils over,
"American" spelled out on the ground.
Her hands are raw,
Her fingers tired,
But this color stain…
Is permanent.

WHAT IS BEAUTY?

The night's canvas after a long rain.
The freshness of it all.
The stars being brighter,
Lighting up the sky.
The purple streaked across the black,
Causing you to stare and wait.
But no, this darkness cannot be beauty,
For beauty is not dark.
But then again,
What is beauty?

The forest at the edge of the city.
Where mystery and evil await.
The forbidden land.
The troubled world.
Where witches and sin prevail.
Or is it just a faraway land?
Looked down upon,
When really the sun shines through.
Where bunnies and bluebirds thrive.

But no, this darkness cannot be beauty,
For beauty is not dark.
But then again,

What is beauty?

A black cat crossing your path,
Dooming you for life.
It's a curse,
A sin,
Bad luck is now thrust upon you.
Or is it just one of God's magnificent creatures,
Strolling through the night?
The moon lighting its way.
But no, this darkness cannot be beauty,
For beauty is not dark.
But then again,
What is beauty?

The brown skin of a Black man;
Tinted by the sun,
Soaking up its warmth and energy.
It's dark chocolate.
Brown sugar.
Cinnamon.
Caramel.
Even a little taste of honey.
All on top of a beautiful sundae.
But no, this darkness cannot be beauty,

For beauty is not dark.
But then again,
What is beauty?

The color "black."
It's ugly,
It's evil,
It's sin,
It's unlucky,
It's death,
It's failure,
It's dark,
It's different,
It's unknown,
But why can't it be beautiful?

The black sky:
It's overwhelming and huge,
But that's the kind of power we can have.
The black forest:
It's a home to many,
But that's what we can provide for others.
The black cat:
A symbol of our mystery,
And of how we are not always what we seem to be.

And black skin:

The epitome of how we take warmth and energy and make things grow.

The color “black,”

Some people view as a threat.

But no…

It’s Beautiful.

The Ripening of the
Fruit

MAN IN THE MIRROR

A Tribute to Michael Jackson, The Greatest Entertainer of All Time

"I'm starting with the *Man in the Mirror*[1]".
Change your ways, man in the mirror.

This little boy that never had the chance to play,
But was forced to see the man in the mirror.

The heart of the world weeps for him.
"The Greatest Entertainer of All Time," the man in the mirror.

Sharing his generosity with the world,
Heal the World like the man in the mirror.

Breaking all the records,
He was one for the books, the man in the mirror.

Passing through barriers as if they were invisible,
He was a first of many, the man in the mirror.

The King of Pop, whose music will never die,
Lives on through admirers, the man in the mirror.

Don't Stop 'Til You Get Enough,
As if anyone ever could of the man in the mirror.

---

[1] Jackson, Michael. "Man in the Mirror." *Bad*, Epic Records, 1988.

I want to *Rock With You*, "share that beat of love[2]",
Thanks to the man in the mirror.

"Live your life *Off the Wall*, let the madness
In the music get to you[3]", man in the mirror.

Want to be Startin' Something?
The intensity is thunderous of the man in the mirror.

Beware of the *Thriller* at night,
He will possess you, the man in the mirror.

Broke out with *Billie Jean* on Motown 25, a night to remember,
Brought the nation to its feet, the man in the mirror.

Tell 'em that it's *Human Nature*, the fight within
To be like our oppressor as did the man in the mirror.

He only wanted to love us
*Pretty Young Thing*s, the man in the mirror.

That was a *Bad* man too, not bad as in bad, but bad as in good.
He was bad. Really, really, bad, the man in the mirror.

---

[2] Jackson, Michael. "Rock With You." *Off the Wall,* Epic Records, 1979.
[3] Jackson, Michael. "Off the Wall." *Off the Wall*, Epic Records, 1979.

Imitators, but never duplicators, he was the
*Smooth*est *Criminal* to walk the earth, the man in the mirror.

The Way You Make Me Feel; this man had everyone jamming,
Even in Budapest, the man in the mirror.

Do you *Remember the Time* when that six-year-old boy
Burst onto the stage with the lungs of life, the man in the mirror.

Following his skin color change, he reminded us,
It doesn't matter if you're *Black or White*, the man in the mirror.

A *Dangerous* man when his voice reached the mic,
When his feet touched the stage, the man in the mirror.

Just upon making the biggest comeback, his unexpected
Departure made you want to scream for the man in the mirror.

"All I want to say is that *They Don't Really Care About Us*[4]",
He was still a brother to our family, the man in the mirror.

But sometimes he felt as if he was all alone and cold inside like a
Stranger in Moscow, locked in a childhood staring at a man in the mirror.

[4] Jackson, Michael. "They Don't Care About Us." *HIStory: Past, Present and Future, Book I*, Epic Records, 1995.

The rumors began to roll,
They told him to *Beat It*, the man in the mirror.

"No one understands me, because I love such elementary things,
But have you seen my *Childhood*?"[5] man in the mirror?

His fans reached out and said, "*You Are Not Alone.*
Though we're far apart, you're always in my heart,"[6] man in the mirror.

This man reached thousands of fans, and inspired hundreds of artists.
His music will always be loved, the man in the mirror.

Despite his skin condition, despite his surgeries, despite his actions,
People loved him for the music that he brought, the man in the mirror.

His music touched the soul of everyone,
And made you grab your heart, the man in the mirror.
Knowing him personally or just knowing his music,
His presence will be dearly missed, the man in the mirror.

---

[5] Jackson, Michael. "Childhood." *HIStory: Past, Present and Future, Book I*, Epic Records, 1995.
[6] Jackson, Michael. "You Are Not Alone." *HIStory: Past, Present and Future, Book I*, Epic Records, 1995.

Rest in peace Michael Joseph Jackson;

August 29th, 1958 to June 25th, 2009.

We hope you are free and more than just, the man in the mirror.

Fly free.

FROM DARKNESS TO LIGHT

Not a trickle of light shone through the darkness,
Even though some swear they saw.
Not a trickle of light shone through the darkness,
Even though it was required by law.

She opens her eyes to darkness each day,
And asks, "When will I shine?"
She opens her eyes to darkness each day,
And asks, "When will everything be fine?"

"We are steadily told that what we want my dear,
Will never come to be.
When all of what we really want my dear,
Is to truly just be me."

"Mommy, when can I walk down the road,
With my eyes to the sky?
Mommy, when can I walk down the road,
With my head held high?"

"Only when Dr. King strolls down the street, my dear,
Can we catch a glimmer of light.
Only when Dr. King strolls down the street, my dear,
Can we get some of the benefits of Whites."

In this day and age, the light,
Glittered between the cracks.
But in this day and age, the light,
Didn't stop some from hidden attacks.

"But mom, I want to be a doctor now,
And the teachers think I cannot.
I'm going to be a doctor now,
And they think I'll end up shot.

You know some of us are beyond McDonald's,
And little old Burger King.
Some of us are beyond McDonald's,
We can achieve anything."

"Just close your eyes and rest your head, my dear,
And you'll be capable of wonders.
Just close your eyes and rest your head, my dear,
The light will strike with great thunder."

She opens her eyes expecting to see the darkness,
But the light has overcome.
She opens her eyes expecting to the see the darkness,
But the light, for once, has won.

The light gracefully dances across the mountains,
Becoming an historic event.

The light gracefully dances across the mountains,
Damn, America has a Black president.

From the darkness,
We were treated no better than dirt,
To the light,
Now we can never be hurt.
From the darkness,
We were dragged to this country in chains,
To the light,
Now we are running the thing.

If it wasn't for Obama,
There would be no 'from darkness to light.'
If it wasn't for Obama,
The barrier's not broken; we would still be in this fight.
If it wasn't for Obama,
True equality would still be deprived.
If it wasn't for Obama,
We would not now have arrived.

From vision to action we walked,
From Kunta Kinte to my mama.
From vision to action we walked,
From Dr. King to Barack Obama.
From vision to action we walked,
From vicious slavery to blessed freedom.

From vision to action we walked,
From the manacles of discrimination, change has finally overcome.

MY EIGHT LETTER WORD
Inspired by Sharon M. Draper's *November Blues*

That eight-letter word that
Changed my life forever.

Funeral.
No. That's seven.
But my boyfriend's still dead…
Anyhow.

Education.
That's nine.
But who knows if I have a
Future
With it.

Change.
That's only six,
But it's something I know all too well of.

How could this eight-letter word
Turn my life inside out and upside down?

How could this happen?
When did this Happen??
…. the night before he died.

This eight-letter word that I cannot bear to whisper.
It makes me vomit,
It makes me dizzy,
It makes me swell
It makes me fat
It makes me feel pain that I've never felt before….
"Mom, I'm —
Pregnant."

Three letter word,
Cry.
I cry for Josh: who will never know what we've created.
I cry for myself: there goes my future down the drain.
I cry for my mom: I was supposed to be her perfect princess.
I cry for the baby: what world are you being born into?

Four letters, Josh.
You left us too soon.
I miss your stupid crooked teeth
And that beaming sunny smile.
I miss the way you made me laugh.
Nothing is the same without you.

Seven letters, Jericho.
Josh's cousin and best friend.
Going from a man whose heart and soul breathed music,

To a man that cannot bear the sound.
He misses you, too.
But a stand-in? Father of our baby?
He offers, but he did not ask for this.
Neither did we, but she's here.

Five letters plus seven. Josh's parents.
They want to take my baby from me.
Give me money for the baby.
Raise it as their own,
Replacing the son they lost.

But – six letters, two words,
This is *my baby*.

This is my baby,
Who I felt move inside of me.
This is my baby,
My beautiful baby girl.
This is my baby,
Who for, I would give up the entire world.
This is my baby,
I instantly loved and cared for her.
This is my baby,
A combination of what we were.
This is my baby,
The one who smiled only for me.

This is my baby,

I know everything will be just fine…

This is my baby, my little eight letter word,

My little Miss –

Sunshine.

FLASHBACK

Extremism in the defense of liberty is no vice.

If one is defending his or her belief, taking extreme actions is acceptable.

America, 2010.

The 21st century.

Inside – Barack Hussein Obama,

The first Black president,

Signed the Healthcare Reform Bill.

Outside – the White mob, red.

N-word, N-word, 15 times.

A brick thrown through the window.

1966. Black Power Movement.

Glass shatters,

We wake up instantly.

Fear stops my heart,

Where are my children?

A brick lands on my kitchen floor.

We duck under our beds and hear,

"Get out of here Nigger!"

A car screeches off into the distance.

America, 2010.

"*Extremism in the defense of liberty is no vice,*"

Was wrapped around the brick.
Barry Goldwater's quote.
Barry Goldwater,
Republican,
1964,
Opposed the Civil Rights Act.

1955. The Era of Segregation.
I step off the bus
And fear strikes my body.
A sea of white stands before me,
Hatred in their eyes.
They yell and throw things;
My body's the target of their aim.
All because I was sitting in the front seat.
A man spit on me,
As if I'm nothing.

2010. A protestor spit
On Black Congressman
Emanuel Cleaver.
Extremism in the defense of liberty is no vice.

1915. Jim Crow.
My feet are bleeding,
My heart is racing,
The dogs are closing in.

Branches are clawing at my face,
I'm sprinting through the black.
"Coon! Coon! We gonna get you!"
What did I do?
What did I say?
The color of my skin explains it all.
Am I gonna die?
There's no questioning it,
Thunder sounds from a rifle.

2010. Sarah Palin.
Don't retreat. Instead…
Reload.
Extremism in the defense of liberty is no vice.

2010. James Clyburn –
Black Congressman, received a fax of a
Noose.
Extremism in the defense of liberty is no vice.

1866. Reconstruction.
Tears stream down my face,
My breathing is short and labored,
I beg him not to go.
But I know it's either him or all of us.
He opens the door.
The fire on the cross

Heats his skin,
The crackling fire burns into my memory,
As he steps past it to the hooded men
By the tree.
"You're always gonna be our slave!" they say,
Tying the knot in the rope.
A noose awaits him.

Slavery abolished.
Fire, Noose, Tar n' Feather, Rape – the Ku Klux Klan.
Extremism, in the defense of liberty, is no vice.
Civil Rights enforced.
Beaten, Hosed, Gassed – Jim Crow.
Extremism, in the defense of liberty, is no vice.
Healthcare reformed.
Threatened, Degraded, Spit on.
Extremism, in the defense of liberty, is no vice….
Extreme acts taken in defense of liberty, is not immoral?

Emancipation Proclamation, 1863.
Civil Rights Act, 1964…
2010. Is this about healthcare reform? Or Barack Obama?

History echoes
To a time where it shouldn't go back.
Are you listening now?

TICK, TOCK…IT'S GRADUATION TIME

There is no stopping the turning of the gears,
That work the grandfather clock – of life.
Childhood, long gone. Adulthood? Approaching.
No slowing down that first – baby – step.
No pausing this: high school graduation.
No grasping, no holding onto the present,
It moves in a blur beyond our control.
We may move slowly, but the clock does not.
One day at a time, becomes a month.
Time waits for no one when we want it to.

Yes, time escapes us,
But what we do with it,
Can either make or break us.
Too many people, cut short in life,
Their dreams never made it.
Don't you be your own knife.
You worked hard to wear that academic gown.
Now anything is possible,
Rise above all who try to hold you down.
The best revenge is to prove them wrong.
Knowledge is power,
And with it, you'll only end up strong.
It's America 2010,
The land of opportunities,

Beginning with your graduation.
So, seize the day,
"Carpe diem"
As they say.

Because you know what, today is a gift;
That's why it's called the present.
Enjoy each hour,
Each minute,
Each second,
Because they make up a lifetime.
Be spontaneous.
Be original.
Be loving.
Be crazy.
Be proper,
Loud
Daring
Classy
Unique
Cuckoo!
Never put life on hold.
Always go for what you want.
The sky is NOT the limit,
Cause there are footprints on the moon!
Don't be the clock focusing on how fast life goes.
Be the compass making sure you're going in the right direction.

But remember, it’s not over.

It’s only…

The beginning.

Tick.

Tock.

Tick.

Tock.

The choice…is yours.

Sweet Cherries and Plums Plucked

Chapter Description

One poem revised four times.

Four times in the span of 5 years.

The same story with different perspectives.

Even though the perspectives were all mine.

As I grew in my identity, culture, and history,

Grew my love for storytelling through imagery.

Ashley Raquelle

THE SLAVE SHIP

I'm in this big canoe boat,

That doesn't seem to stay afloat.

Water leaks in,

And it's very, very dim.

We're all crammed in here like spoons,

Being shipped far away to our doom.

The Whites chain us together so we don't up-rise,

And the only time you get some space is if the person beside you dies.

All of us are starving down here,

And if you look in our eyes, you see fear.

Some people are sick, some people are sore,

And a lot of us are lying on the floor.

They feed us watery rice,

And shave our heads to be free from lice.

I'm all alone,

And I can't go home.

None of us speak the same,

The person beside me doesn't even know my name.

I feel like I want to die,

But I just sit here and cry.

I'll never see my family again,

And if I do who knows when.

I am only thirteen,

And these White people are really, really mean.

My people also get whipped,

And this is what happened on

The Slave Ship!

SLAVE SHIP VERSION 2

I am suddenly in this big canoe boat,
That seems to be having problems staying afloat.

Through every crack and cranny, water leaks in.
There is hardly any light; it is very, very dim.

We're all crammed up tight together like spoons,
Being shipped far away to our possible doom.

The Whites chain us together so we don't up-rise,
And the only time you get some space is if someone dies.

We are starving down here,
And our eyes show nothing but fear.

Some people are sick, some people are sore,
but all of us are chained to this floor.

They feed us nothing but watery rice,
And shave our heads to keep from becoming infested with lice.

I am here in the dark and all alone.
What chance do I have to ever go home?

Only some of us speak the same,
None of us even know each other's names.

I am so tired and hurt that I want to die,
But all I can do is lie here and cry.

I'll probably never see my family again.
And if I ever do, who even knows when.

I am frightened, scared, and only thirteen,
And these White devils are really, really mean.

Every day many of us get whipped,
This is now the only life we know on the
Slave Ship!

SLAVE SHIP TAKE 3

I'm scared.
I cannot breathe.
There is no air,
Just darkness.

I awoke to the smell of blood and tears,
With people screaming around me.
Seawater and puke fall onto my face,
I am left in the filth for days.
They feed us this watery rice,
But every time I eat it, my stomach comes up into my mouth.
My ankles and wrists bleed as the chains dig into my skin.
The wood that I lay on gnaws at my back,
Setting it on fire.

I don't know what to do,
I was snatched away from my family.
I'm all alone in this big canoe boat.
People shout, but I don't understand their words.
All I do is lie here and cry.
I don't want to live like this,
Chained up,
Barely feed,
Treated like cattle,

Where is Allah?

Why does he not help me?

I don’t want to live like this,

I just want to die.

THE NIGHTMARE THAT WAS REALITY: MEMORIES OF THE MIDDLE PASSAGE

I slowly blink open my eyes
As if in a dream.
But light never comes.
I try to sit up;
A sharp pain pierces through my shoulders,
My head begins to thump.
I try to reach for my head,
My hand never comes.
It's chained down to the wood plank beneath me.

My heart begins to race
As questions fill my mind.
Other sounds start to swim into my ears,
I hear crying, groaning, screaming.
My whole-body shakes with fear.

My eyes adjust to the darkness –
Hundreds of bodies lay around me.
I squirm trying to get away.
The chains scrape against my wrists and ankles
Leaving a trail of blood behind.
The wood gnaws at my back
Tearing away some skin.

It’s loud.
I don’t understand anyone’s words.
Where’s my mother?

I feel hot breath on my neck
From the person beside me.
I stare into the eyes of the other,
They don’t blink.

I try to take gulps of air,
But I find there is none.
Only the smell of sweat,
Vomit,
Urination,
Defecation.
My throat tightens from thirst.

The pale faces come down,
Yanking us up,
Striking our feet if we don’t cooperate.
Once up top, the sun blinds us.
Water surrounds us on all sides.
Where is my home?
Where is my family?

I glance at the pale faces
With their knives,
Whips,
And black steel objects.
There are great fish with gray fins
Waiting in the water below…

I look to the sky,
I hear a voice,
And He tells me…
"I haven't failed you yet."

ABOUT THE POET

MY STORY AS A WRITER

Raquelle A. Smartt, a Maryland native known by her pen name *Ashley Raquelle*, loved to read and write from a young age. Transforming the stories she played out with her Barbie dolls into words for a class assignment at the age of eight, she began her writing journey. Though, it was not until middle school that she would discover her love for poetry and the emotional imagery of language.

In the summer of 2006, Ashley Raquelle attended the Student Writers' Workshop. Stepping outside of school to learn the skills and artistry of creative writing, this showed her commitment to her craft.

In 10th grade, Raquelle joined the school newspaper. Expanding her writing beyond fiction and poetry, she began to focus on the Black American experience that had always been close to her heart. At her majority White high school, she wrote an op-ed about the psychological effects of slavery. This was only the beginning of Raquelle using her voice as an activist to speak out against discrimination; (be it racism, sexism, xenophobia, homophobia, etc.). She also used her voice as an advocate for the causes she believed in.

In 2009, she was one of the 19th Annual Rev. Dr. Martin Luther King Jr. Written Expression Award Winners for her poem,

"From Darkness to Light," which she performed at the Theodore W. Stephens Honors Awards Program held by the Frederick Alumni Chapter of Kappa Alpha Psi Fraternity. The call and response of performing her poetry and connecting with the audience as her words, message, and meaning impacted them would speak to her spirit.

In the summer of 2009, Raquelle attended Firespark! at Brenau University, a 2-week summer camp where she took classes in poetry, fiction, and print journalism from professional writers. It was here that she decided not to pursue print journalism in college, but instead to use her empowering voice and past acting skills to enter into the field of broadcast journalism.

Raquelle won first place in the 2010 Frederick Co. Public Schools Literacy Fair for her poem "My Eight Letter Word." It was inspired by the Maryland Black-Eyed Susan novel *November Blues* by Sharon M. Draper. Sharon M. Draper along with Mildred D. Taylor and Sharon G. Flake were her favorite authors as a teen. As an adult, La Jill Hunt was added to the list. Realistic fiction, historical fiction, and dystopian literature centering transitional age youth were the genres of novels she loved to read and to write.

Raquelle held the honor of performing her poem, "Tick, Tock...It's Graduation Time" at her High School Graduation. With multiple performances and awards by the end of high school, Ashley Raquelle had secured herself as a writer.

Raquelle attended and graduated from Hampton University with a Bachelor of Arts degree in Broadcast Journalism and minors in English and Psychology. After taking a Black Psychology class for fun, her fascination with the mind, relationships, and the psychosocial effects of being Black in America expanded her career path. Raquelle interned with Hampton's *WHOV* 88.1 FM radio station and *WHRO* Public Media on the *Cathy Lewis Show*. After the incredible opportunity of speaking live with the audience and also producing a show, she got the idea of becoming a radio psychologist or talk show therapist. Raquelle had always loved listening to talk radio growing up, especially the *Russ Parr Morning Show*, the *Tom Joyner Morning Show*, and the *Steve Harvey Morning Show*.

While exploring these other interests and after experiencing some personal trauma, Raquelle took a two-year break from creatively writing; the first time since she started. In 2013, she returned and won first place in the Poetry Society of Virginia 2013 Student Contest - Category S-8 for her poem "Great Spirit Gaia."

Combining her interests of writing and relationships, Raquelle interned at *YourTango*, an online relationship magazine. There she got the opportunity to read, edit, and optimize articles from experts in the field she was entering.

Raquelle went on to obtain her Master of Arts degree in Marital and Family Therapy from the University of San Diego. She became a Licensed Marriage and Family Therapist, a Clinical Supervisor, a Sister Circle Facilitator, and a Happiness Coach at Manifest Realities Happiness Coaching.

She also began a podcast, the *It'sSoulReal Podcast*, with her now husband who is also a LMFT, where they challenge societal norms, deconstruct the reality we live in, and question our thinking processes.

Ashley Raquelle had her first paid poetry performance in 2021 with her poem "The Black Woman is God" at the graduation ceremony for the Oakland/Bay Area cohort of the Sisters Mentally Mobilized Advocate Training Program within California Black Women's Health Project.

In 2022, she returned to her original art form of fiction. In the *Something or Other Publishing*'s Second Annual Short Story Contest, she was both the first prize winner in the young adult category and the Curator's Choice Award Winner for her short story "White Walls."

Raquelle has now lived in California for the past ten years and currently reflects on life, relationships, and womanhood on her Facebook blog and YouTube channel, *LifeIsRocqi*. She is still performing her poetry with videos now available on her YouTube channel. She has also begun exploring abstract acrylic painting. Raquelle hopes to write self-help books and workbooks in the future as well as continue to publish her books of poetry.

Raquelle has dedicated her life to helping others, using her voice to inspire, and being unapologetically Black while doing so.

"Activism is the rent I pay for living on this planet."

Alice Walker

"A waterfall begins with a single drop of water."

Ashley Raquelle

www.ingramcontent.com/pod-product-compliance
Lightning Source LLC
LaVergne TN
LVHW050541100826
845148LV00002B/640